■ SCHOLASTIC

MULTIPLICATION x HOUSES x

By Violet Findley

D1708067

NEW YORK • TORONTO • LONDON • AUCKLAND • SYDNEY
MEXICO CITY • NEW DELHI • HONG KONG • BUENOS AIRES

Teaching *Resources*

Cover and interior design by Brian LaRossa
Illustration by Doug Jones

ISBN: 978-0-545-29294-8

Welcome to *Multiplication Houses*! Research shows that mastering the multiplication facts from 0 to 12 is a very effective way to boost math fluency and meet the NCTM Standards. (See Meeting the Standards on page 5.) But committing the facts to memory can be quite an undertaking for children. That's where this innovative resource comes in! It's packed with 20-plus open-n-peek "multiplication houses" that make learning each fact family easy and entertaining. Because these manipulatives are self-correcting, students can use them independently. And because they include riddles, you can be certain students will turn to them again and again with a positive attitude toward memorizing the tables.

Making the Manipulatives

To make the multiplication houses, gather these materials and follow the directions below.

Materials

- house patterns (2 pages)
- scissors or craft knife (NOTE: Craft knife to be used by adults only.)
- crayons or markers
- glue stick

Directions

1. Copy the top and bottom of a multiplication house pattern onto paper or cardstock as shown below.

2. Color both sheets, or invite children to color them.

3. Cut out both patterns along the dashed gray lines. Cut out the window and door openings along the dashed lines as well.

4. Add glue to the back pattern around the window frames and door.

5. Affix the top pattern to the bottom pattern, so the windows open onto the multiplication-sentence answers and the door opens onto the riddle answer.

6. Optional: Laminate each multiplication house for added durability.

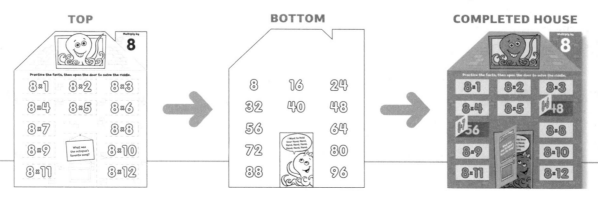

Using the Manipulatives

Inside this book, you'll find a different multiplication house for each fact family, from 0 to 12. You will also find six mixed-fact multiplication houses (for added practice) and two blank multiplication houses, which can be customized to review any facts you choose. There is a multitude of ways to use these engaging manipulatives including:

1. **Meaningful Seatwork:** Provide all students with a personal set of multiplication houses, encouraging kids to use them first thing in the morning or between assignments.

2. **Center-Time Activity:** Color and laminate the multiplication houses, then place them on a designated "Multiplication-Table Table" for kids to explore—and master—during center time.

3. **Hands-On Homework:** Send home a different multiplication house each week and instruct students to use it for five minutes a night with the goal of mastering a given fact family by the end of the week.

MEETING THE STANDARDS

The hands-on learning tools in this book will help you meet the following essential Grades 3 to 5 National Council of Teachers of Mathematics (NCTM) standards:

Compute fluently and make reasonable estimates

- develop fluency with basic number combinations for multiplication and division and use these combinations to mentally compute related problems

- develop fluency in adding, subtracting, multiplying, and dividing whole numbers

- develop and use strategies to estimate the results of whole-number computations and to judge the reasonableness of such results

---

Multiply by

0

I have
0 legs!

Practice the facts, then open the door to solve the riddle.

0 x 1

0 x 2

0 x 3

0 x 4

0 x 5

0 x 6

0 x 7

0 x 8

0 x 9

What
do ghosts
eat for lunch?

0 x 10

0 x 11

0 x 12

0   0   0

0   0   0

0   0

0   BOO-logna   0
      sandwiches!

0   0

Multiply by

1

I have 1 tail!

Practice the facts, then open the door to solve the riddle.

1 x 1   1 x 2   1 x 3

1 x 4   1 x 5   1 x 6

1 x 7   1 x 8

1 x 9   Why do snakes love to tell jokes?   1 x 10

1 x 11   1 x 12

1

2

3

4

5

6

7

8

9

10

11

12

Multiply by

2

I have 2 eyes!

Practice the facts, then open the door to solve the riddle.

2 × 1   2 × 2   2 × 3

2 × 4   2 × 5   2 × 6

2 × 7   2 × 8

2 × 9   2 × 10

Why are snails such good employees?

2 × 11   2 × 12

2   4   6

8   10   12

14   16

Because
we are always
on slime!

18   20

22   24

Multiply by

3

Practice the facts, then open the door to solve the riddle.

3 x 1

3 x 2

3 x 3

3 x 4

3 x 5

3 x 6

3 x 7

3 x 8

3 x 9

Why did the clown take his nose off?

3 x 10

3 x 11

3 x 12

3   6   9

12   15   18

21   24

27   30

33   36

Multiply by
4

I have 4 spots!

Practice the facts, then open the door to solve the riddle.

4 × 1   4 × 2   4 × 3

4 × 4   4 × 5   4 × 6

4 × 7   4 × 8

4 × 9   What do cows do for fun?   4 × 10

4 × 11   4 × 12

4

8

12

16

20

24

28

32

36

40

44

48

Multiply by 5

I have 5 arms!

Practice the facts, then open the door to solve the riddle.

5×1 5×2 5×3

5×4 5×5 5×6

5×7 5×8

5×9 5×10

What kind of fish loves to sign autographs?

5×11 5×12

5   10   15

20   25   30

35   40

45   50

55   60

I have 6 spots!

Multiply by 6

Practice the facts, then open the door to solve the riddle.

6 x 1	6 x 2	6 x 3
6 x 4	6 x 5	6 x 6
6 x 7		6 x 8
6 x 9	Where are ladybugs not welcome?	6 x 10
6 x 11		6 x 12

6 12 18

24 30 36

42 48

The men's room!

54 60

66 72

I have 7 plates on my back!

Multiply by

7

Practice the facts, then open the door to solve the riddle.

7 x 1

7 x 2

7 x 3

7 x 4

7 x 5

7 x 6

7 x 7

7 x 8

7 x 9

What do you call a sleeping dinosaur?

7 x 10

7 x 11

7 x 12

7   14   21

28   35   42

49   56

A stego-SNORE-ous!

63   70

77   84

Multiply by

8

I have 8 arms!

Practice the facts, then open the door to solve the riddle.

8 x 1

8 x 2

8 x 3

8 x 4

8 x 5

8 x 6

8 x 7

8 x 8

8 x 9

What is an octopus's favorite song?

8 x 10

8 x 11

8 x 12

8   16   24

32   40   48

56   64

I Want to Hold
Your Hand, Hand,
Hand, Hand, Hand,
Hand, Hand, Hand.

72   80

88   96

Multiply by

9

I have 9 bubbles!

Practice the facts, then open the door to solve the riddle.

9 x 1   9 x 2   9 x 3

9 x 4   9 x 5   9 x 6

9 x 7   9 x 8

9 x 9   Why did the fish cross the ocean?   9 x 10

9 x 11   9 x 12

9   18   27

36   45   54

63   72

81   90

He wanted to get to the other tide!

99   108

Multiply by 10

I have 10 feathers!

Practice the facts, then open the door to solve the riddle.

10 × 1	10 × 2	10 × 3
10 × 4	10 × 5	10 × 6
10 × 7		10 × 8

Why did the turkey jump out of the plane with a parachute?

| 10 × 9 | | 10 × 10 |
| 10 × 11 | | 10 × 12 |

10   20   30

40   50   60

70   80

90   100

110   120

Multiply by

11

I have 11 stripes on my back!

Practice the facts, then open the door to solve the riddle.

11 x 1

11 x 2

11 x 3

11 x 4

11 x 5

11 x 6

11 x 7

11 x 8

11 x 9

What is a tiger's favorite food?

11 x 10

11 x 11

11 x 12

11   22   33

44   55   66

77   88

99   110

121   132

Multiply by

12

I have 12 teeth!

Practice the facts, then open the door to solve the riddle.

12 × 1   12 × 2   12 × 3

12 × 4   12 × 5   12 × 6

12 × 7   12 × 8

12 × 9   What are alligators always wearing?   12 × 10

12 × 11   12 × 12

12   24   36

48   60   72

84   96

108      120

132   144

Multiply by
1&2

Practice the facts, then open the door to solve the riddle.

1 x 2   2 x 2   1 x 3

2 x 4   1 x 5   2 x 12

1 x 7

Why do cats love to take tests?

2 x 8

2 x 6   1 x 9

2   4   3

8   5   24

7   16

12   9

We always get a PURRR-fect score!

Multiply by
3&4

Practice the facts, then open the door to solve the riddle.

4 × 11   3 × 2   4 × 9

3 × 8   4 × 5   3 × 6

4 × 7   Why do farm animals like living near horses?   3 × 4

4 × 4   3 × 10

44   6   36

24   20   18

28      12

16   30

Practice the facts, then open the door to solve the riddle.

5 x 1   **6 x 8**   **5 x 4**

6 x 9   **5 x 5**   **6 x 6**

5 x 7   What is a mouse's very favorite magazine?   **6 x 2**

5 x 9   **6 x 10**

5   48   20

54   25   36

35      12

45   60

Multiply by
7&8

Practice the facts, then open the door to solve the riddle.

7×10   7×2   8×4

7×11   8×5   7×6

8×3   What kind of music do bunnies love?   7×8

8×9   8×1

70   14   32

77   40   42

24   Hip-Hop!   56

72   8

Multiply by
9&10

Practice the facts, then open the door to solve the riddle.

10x1 **9x2** **10x4**

10x5 **9x9** **9x6**

10x3

Where do sheep put their money?

9x8

10x9

9x7

10   18   40

50   81   54

30   In the BAAA-nk!   72

$ DEPOSIT SLIP

90   63

Multiply by

11&12

Practice the facts, then open the door to solve the riddle.

12×8   12×2   11×4

12×9   11×5   12×6

11×3   What is the spider's favorite activity?   11×1

11×9   12×7

96   24   44

108   55   72

33      11

99   84

Multiply by

Practice the facts, then open the door to solve the riddle.

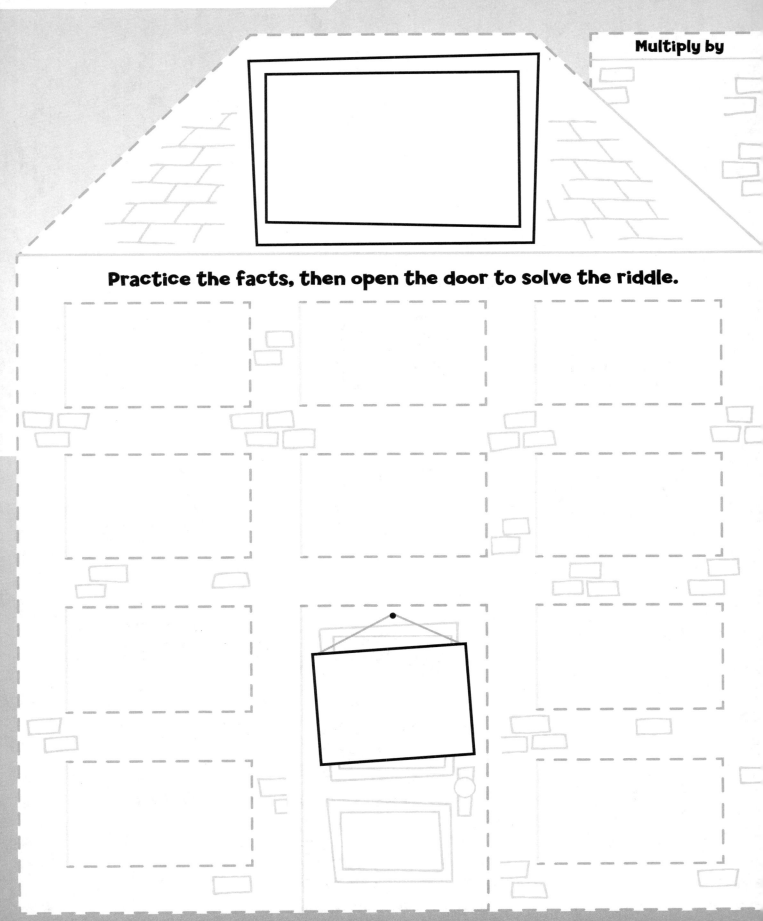

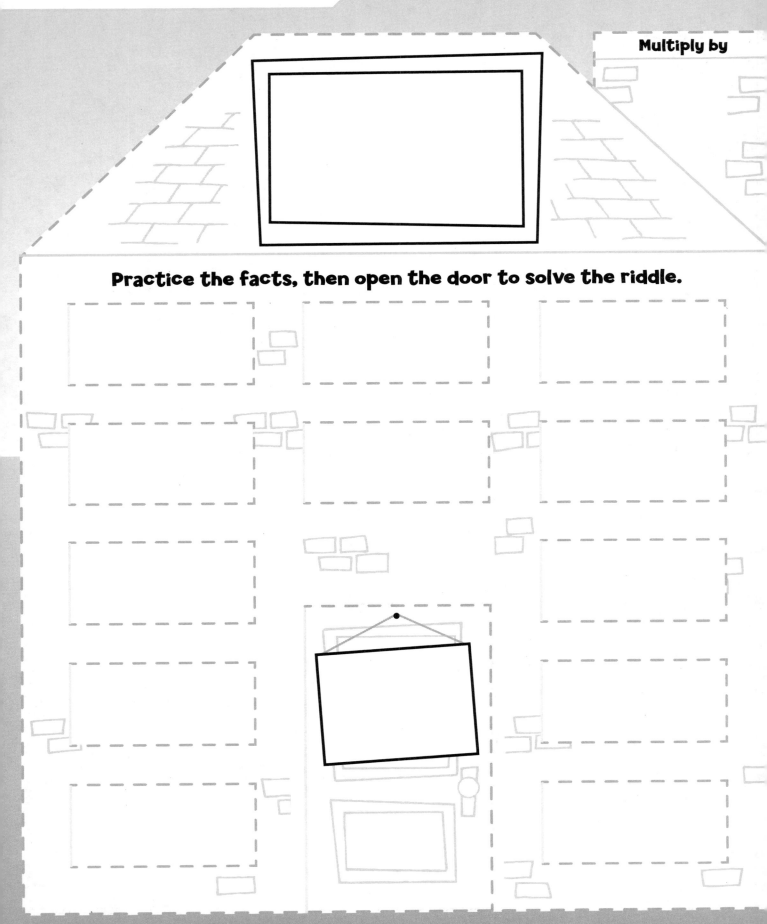

Multiply by

Practice the facts, then open the door to solve the riddle.

FACT TABLE 1–12

x	0	1	2	3	4	5	6	7	8	9	10	11	12
0	0	0	0	0	0	0	0	0	0	0	0	0	0
1	0	1	2	3	4	5	6	7	8	9	10	11	12
2	0	2	4	6	8	10	12	14	16	18	20	22	24
3	0	3	6	9	12	15	18	21	24	27	30	33	36
4	0	4	8	12	16	20	24	28	32	36	40	44	48
5	0	5	10	15	20	25	30	35	40	45	50	55	60
6	0	6	12	18	24	30	36	42	48	54	60	66	72
7	0	7	14	21	28	35	42	49	56	63	70	77	84
8	0	8	16	24	32	40	48	56	64	72	80	88	96
9	0	9	18	27	36	45	54	63	72	81	90	99	108
10	0	10	20	30	40	50	60	70	80	90	100	110	120
11	0	11	22	33	44	55	66	77	88	99	110	121	132
12	0	12	24	36	48	60	72	84	96	108	120	132	144